WE ALL SHARE

Introducing Holy Communion to under 5s
through play, exploration and creativity

Mina Munns

**kevin
mayhew**

kevin
mayhew

First published in Great Britain in 2018 by Kevin Mayhew Ltd
Buxhall, Stowmarket, Suffolk IP14 3BW
Tel: +44 (0) 1449 737978 Fax: +44 (0) 1449 737834
E-mail: info@kevinmayhew.com

www.kevinmayhew.com

9 8 7 6 5 4 3 2 1 0

ISBN 978 1 84867 939 9
Catalogue No. 1501576

Cover design by Rob Mortonson
© Images used under licence from Shutterstock Inc.
Typeset by Rob Mortonson
Printed and bound in Great Britain

Contents

Acknowledgements

Thanks to everyone who helped me to put this book together, but especially to Catherine Ward who started me off on this track and to Melody Briggs who helped me to sort out my initial jumble of thoughts on this topic!

Thanks must also go to all those who contributed their stories and experiences: Rebecca Marriott, Emma Fyffe, Rob Clements, Carolynn Pritchard, Helen Hooley, Amanda Lees, Traci Smith, Andy Stinson, Sharon Lord, Anna Alls, Olivia A. J. Haines, Vicki Evans, Marie-Pierre Tonnon-Louant, Jemma Allen, Ally Barrett, Alex Sanderson, Karen Ware-Jackson, Bonnie Thomson, Kate Mitchell, Nicole Hall, Judy Heron-Graham, Lisa Marie, Ramona Samuel, Craig and Caroline Prest, Marcus Hockley, Martha Hubbard Miller, Rachel Shilling, Victoria Beech.

I am very grateful to Fr Simon Rundell for letting us include part of his Nursery Rhyme Mass liturgy and to my friends Paula Daley, Helen Ward, Kirstine Buchan and James Pacey for reading through the draft version of this book and for their encouragement.

About the Author

Mina Munns is an Anglican priest in the Diocese of Southwell and Nottingham. She is a former primary school teacher and church children's worker and has a particular interest in children's prayer and spirituality. Mina writes the craft page for *Premier Youth and Children's Work Magazine* and, in addition to blogging at Flame Creative Children's Ministry, she maintains The Well: Creative Children's Ministry blog for children's leaders in the Methodist Church. She also runs workshops at gatherings of children's work leaders across the country.

http://flamecreativekids.blogspot.co.uk

https://methodistchildrencreativeministry.org

Introduction

I have to be honest and admit that when I first started working as a church children's worker, the under 5s were not my main interest or priority. Having trained as a primary school teacher, I then spent seven years teaching junior children in the 7-11s age range. I had never really ventured into Key Stage 1, let alone the nursery! When I started working for the church, I had virtually no experience with children under 5 and I was quite happy to let the crèche team carry on as they had been doing with the 0-2s, while I concentrated on writing and resourcing materials for the 3-11s. This at least was an age bracket I understood.

A year or so into my job, I was approached by a mother from our congregation who was volunteering to be on our crèche team. We went out for a coffee to chat about it and that is the moment things really began to change my outlook on children's ministry. Catherine was studying for a degree in Early Years Education and was really enthusiastic to try out in our Sunday morning crèche some of what she had been learning. Having no real sense of expertise myself, I was more than happy to let her experiment.

As I saw what was happening, I became more and more excited and enthused myself and, soon, hanging out in crèche on a Sunday morning became one of my favourite things. As Catherine and the team developed a real sense of God's love for children and parents in the crèche, and provided open-ended, exploratory and sensory activities, through which children could experience awe and wonder and find out more about the amazing world around them, I became more and more aware of the extraordinary spiritual depth of our youngest children. Soon we had developed a vision for our children's ministry that focused on asking questions, exploring independently and deepening relationships with God and with each other. Importantly, the vision included children from the smallest babies, and the playful, sensory steps towards God which children encountered in crèche and in our 3-5s group were stepping stones to the ways in which we explored God with children as they got older.

My interest in the spirituality of the under 5s and their importance as members of the church grew and developed as I journeyed in my own vocation. As part of my ordination training I was fortunate enough to be able to study the links between play and spiritual growth. This book stems from a project I undertook to explore the ways in which children under 5 could be included in the Anglican Eucharistic liturgy through play. It was important for me to find ways in which even the very youngest could be included in the meal that unites us as a Christian family and tells an amazing story about who we are as a community. If we truly believe that children are part of the church, then we must make sure they can connect as fully as possible with the story and actions of one of our most important rituals.

In putting this book together I have been really blessed by contributions from clergy and children's ministry practitioners across denominations and across the world. It has been fascinating to discover their stories and to hear again and again how deeply our under 5s can connect with God. May you be similarly inspired as you read.

Chapter 1

Under 5s and Worship

For those of us fortunate enough to have children under 5 in our congregations, there is often a range of issues to consider – not least the question of our ability to provide for them as worshipping members of our family. While many churches offer Sunday school or Junior church for school-age children, provision for the youngest in our midst is often variable or non-existent. For various understandable reasons, including lack of facilities and volunteers, some churches are unable to provide care for the under 5s age group during a service, yet the missional and evangelistic potential of including all ages within a worship context cannot be denied. To look at the Church of England alone, a survey taken 10 years ago indicates that 47 per cent of church attenders had an average age of 65 plus.[1] The church is getting older and it seems to be the case that we need to reach younger if we want to grow.

The need for growth, though, is not the only reason for exploring our provision for children under 5. If we fail to meet their needs as worshippers, then we are doing them as much a disservice as we would be if we ignored the needs of their parents or grandparents. When Jesus rebuked the disciples and said 'Let the little children come to me, and do not stop them; for it is to such as these that the kingdom of heaven belongs.' (Matthew 19:14) he was not joking. Jesus was making a point about the value of those we might sometimes see as lesser considerations: the poor, the weak, the children. Those who we, perhaps, overlook in our understanding of what is most important when we come to worship have as much value in the eyes of God as any adult worshipper.

 ## Worshipping with under 5s

In any exploration of worship, we probably first need to establish what we mean by worship. For many, the default when we talk about worship is music or singing, but this is only a fraction of the truth. It's easy to see why young children especially might disengage from 'worship' if it is largely seen in verbal

1. http://www.churchgrowthresearch.org.uk/statistics_age_profile

terms – singing and speaking. Working with under 5s means we often have to come from an angle that addresses something more multi-sensory. We need to ask ourselves where the visual and kinesthetic aspect of worship can be tapped into. Where are the colours, textures, tastes, smells and actions of worship for those who might be at a preverbal stage? How can we open up the definition of worship so that all, even the youngest, can be included on their own terms?

Case Study 1: Flags, St Mary's, Westwood

Our church has an extended time of worship during the morning service – usually consisting of about three songs played back to back. During this time some of the children (and a couple of the adults!) like to dance with flags. We have a large collection of these in various sizes and colours and children can freely access them when they want to. One Sunday, Albert (aged 12 months) was at the back, being held in his mother's arms. He was watching the flags move over his head and was obviously very taken by the colours. One of the adults offered one of the smaller flags to Albert and he readily grabbed hold of it, waving it with great delight for the rest of the worship time. His flag waving was obviously related to the music he was hearing and it was wonderful to see the absorbed expression on his face as his flag joined with the colours of the others.

Morgan, aged 3, had long resisted the flags, preferring to read a book in the children's area or to sit with his parents. After at least a year of trying to interest him, I turned around during one service to see that he had chosen one of the larger flags and was waving it very seriously with the music. I exchanged a look with his parents, who had spotted him and were smiling but had obviously chosen to let him get on with it without comment. It was a significant moment because it felt as if Morgan had chosen independently when and how he wanted to participate in worship.

Case Study 2: Worship Station, St Mary's, Westwood

As a smaller church, there are certain weeks when we are unable to provide an organised children's group because we just don't have the volunteers available. We have been investigating ways of including the children (mainly children in the 3-7 age range) in the service so that they can truly be part of what we are doing.

One of our experiments has been to provide a couple of tables and some chairs that the children have free access to, so that they can come and go as they please. The tables have been moved to the front by the lectern, from their original spot at the back of church. This was a deliberate move to make the children visible as part of the church family and to show that they are not to be 'hidden' at the back. Children can choose to come to the tables, dance with flags or stay with their parents.

On the tables we put a variety of activities, all loosely connected to the service theme, that the children can choose from: play dough mats, colouring sheets, sticking crafts, jigsaws. This has gradually become the children's 'own space' where they are happy to sit and use what is on the table without adult intervention, though the service leader or another adult often sits with them during musical worship or the sermon slot, again to show that the children are valued as members of the congregation. It has been wonderful to observe 3 and 4-year-olds actively engaging with service materials, coming and going to share what they are doing with their parents, and being part of worship on independent terms.

The capacity of children under 5 to be true worshippers is often vastly underestimated by adults. There is no doubt that, from the earliest age, children are beginning to connect with God and to explore what worship means – often in very individual ways. Educator Maria Montessori was a firm believer that the period before the age of 6 was the time of the 'absorbent mind' [2]

2. Maria Montessori, *Teaching religion to young children* in Standing, E. M., (Ed.), *The Child in the Church*, (St Paul: Catechetical Guild Educational Society, 1965), page 57.

and various commentators on child faith development, including James Fowler and Jerome Berryman (the creator of Godly Play) have attested to the fact that the journey in faith begins from babyhood. The case studies above illustrate children demonstrating joy in active worship and the importance of independence and choice in coming to God, even at such an early age. Worship is not worship if it is forced upon a child, but we as adults do have the ability to be facilitators and providers of opportunity in a worship context.

Linking education practice to worship exploration

One of the most fascinating things we can do as facilitators of worship with children under 5 is to investigate what is going on in the educational world and use the knowledge and expertise in that field to inform and energise our own practice. Many of our children are, after all, likely to be spending a chunk of their weekly lives in nurseries and preschools and it makes sense to borrow and build on ideas that have been tried and tested in those settings, so that we can tap into a sense of continuity and familiarity. Just as education moves on and nurseries today are unlikely to be the same as nurseries 30 years ago, our practice in church must also move on and take what is good from other settings. We must not be afraid to learn from those outside the church.

Case Study 3: Catherine Ward, St Nic's, Nottingham

I worked with Mina leading the Sunday morning crèche group at St Nic's at the same time as I was studying for a degree in education, specialising in early years. I was privileged to be able to use what I was learning at university and consider how educational practice would work in a church context.

One of the things that really inspired me was the work of Elinor Goldschmeid and Sonia Jackson and their ideas of treasure baskets and heuristic play. Treasure baskets are intended for babies who can sit comfortably but are not yet mobile and are a delightful collection of natural and household objects made from wood, leather and cloth.

Ours has coasters, pieces of cedar wood, little samples of knitting, short lengths of ribbon, a leather bookmark, various brushes, a wooden nutcracker and lots, lots more. The idea is to allow babies to sit, often together, one either side of the treasure basket and explore, with all their senses, all the items in the basket. As a Christian who believes in a creator God, I really feel that there is some great worth in sharing something of the variety of creation, using the natural materials that you collect for a treasure basket, with the very youngest children in church.

Heuristic play is intended for slightly older children and again is really focused on exploration. Toddlers are offered collections of tins, boxes, ribbons, clothes pegs, mug trees, kitchen roll holders, napkin rings, bangles, curtain rings . . . the list goes on. If given time and space toddlers will post, hang, loop, hide and slot the pieces together in a new way every time. There is no end product, no outcome which has been predetermined by a grown-up. It is exploration for its own sake, and whilst I can sit alongside children and show interest in what they are doing, I don't get to choose what is explored or created.

Where we have offered children ideas about God to consider, we have linked those to items that the children could explore in their own way. When we spent our five minutes of carpet time talking, reading and singing about God as creator we offered the interesting tastes and textures of a variety of fruit as well as other natural materials throughout the rest of the session. When we told the story of the wise and foolish builders, we let the children spend lots of time exploring how they might build with blocks (another lovely, open-ended resource). Although we suspected (and indeed hoped) that our under 3s would not understand the themes of pain, humiliation, sin and death that exist within the Easter story, we asked ourselves what they would understand and we collected love hearts in the form of tins, dishes, cookie cutters and Christmas tree decorations, allowed the children time to explore them with the heuristic play things and then sang 'Jesus' love is very wonderful' at carpet time.

I love the idea of this exploration as the beginning of a theme which runs right though our church children's work.
As a parent, as well as an early years educator and a crèche leader, I love the idea of church as a place where my daughter can ask questions, be herself, and meditate upon the mysteries of faith as well as learn scripture.

The guidelines published for the Early Years Foundation Stage (EYFS) have underpinning themes that could, indeed, have been written with faith communities in mind. They express what we, as a church family, should surely be seeking to provide for each of our children: recognising the 'uniqueness' of each child, providing 'positive relationships' and 'enabling environments' and recognising their differing needs as they grow towards independence.[3] Above all, these guidelines advocate the concept that years 0-5 of a child's life are key to laying the foundations for their future. What we do with our youngest children now and how we enable them to explore and interact with God will sow the seeds of their future faith journey and this cannot be underestimated.

If we are serious about helping children to explore worship and to become fully part of the church's body, then we could do worse than borrow from these values in our work with under 5s. Young children are beginning to get an idea of what God is like from their earliest interactions. We, as adults, can be positive role models of love, care and challenge as we help them to discover him more deeply.

Play and worship

From an educational standpoint, theories vary as to how exactly play and learning are linked, yet the connection is a strong one. Through play, children have the opportunity to explore, create and recreate the world they see around them. They engage with the imagination and bring about new possibilities. While in school children might play in the 'home corner' and explore aspects of family and home life they see played out on a daily basis, in church it is easy to imagine that the same might apply to a 'worship corner'. As they observe,

3. Department for Education, Statutory Framework for the Early Years Foundation Stage: Setting the Standards for Learning, Development and Care for Children from Birth to Five, (Crown Copyright, 2017), page 6.

play and explore what they see happening around them in church and other Christian contexts, children have the chance to learn more about elements of worship and to connect with God in incredibly creative ways. Peter Privett puts it succinctly when he says that play 'is not only a creative opportunity, it is a prophetic opening, a Kairos moment of new beginning'.[4] In play, it is possible to argue, children are able to worship and respond to the Creator creatively and naturally and to discover more of the 'new' about self, Christian community, God and the world.

Let's hold on to that idea of Kairos moments as we move to think more specifically about helping our under 5s to engage in and worship as part of Holy Communion.

Useful books

- **The Spiritual Guidance of Children: Montessori, Godly Play and the Future**
  Jerome Berryman, (New York: Morehouse Publishing, 2013).

- **Stages of Faith: The Psychology of Human Development and the Quest for Meaning**
  James W. Fowler, (New York: Harper One, 1981).

- **Through the Eyes of a Child: New Insights in Theology from a Child's Perspective**
  Anne Richards and Peter Privett (Eds.)
  (London: Church House Publishing, 2009).

Useful websites

- **Godventure:** www.godventure.co.uk

- **Worshiping with children:** www.worshipingwithchildren.blogspot.co.uk

- **Karen Ware Jackson:** www.karenwarejackson.com

---

4. Peter Privett, *Play* in Richards, Anne and Privett, Peter (Eds.), *Through the Eyes of a Child: New Insights in Theology from a Child's Perspective,* (London: Church House Publishing, 2009), page 121.

Chapter 2

Under 5s aNd COMMuNioN

The inclusion of children within Holy Communion (or the Mass, Eucharist or Lord's Supper, depending on your tradition) is approached in a variety of ways across each denomination. Some denominations will require baptism and perhaps further preparation as a prerequisite for receiving the bread and wine, while others, who practise believer's baptism of adults or teenagers, will allow younger children to receive if parents are satisfied that they understand the significance of what they are doing.

While we are not attempting, here, to add a voice to the debate over whether children under 5 should receive Communion, we will explore practical thoughts and ideas as to how they might be included, at an age-appropriate level, in the story of what is happening when we celebrate Communion. Sharing the bread and wine is, after all, one of the most important things Jesus commands his disciples to do and it is an incredibly meaningful symbol of our belonging to the body of Christ. Every time we come to Communion we tell, through the words of story or liturgy or a brief recount of 1 Corinthians 11:23-26, what happened at the Last Supper and it is to this story that we all, whatever our age, belong. Our exploration here of how play and creativity can connect children with this story, is a way of helping them to experience and familiarise themselves with the themes, actions, sights, words and feelings of Communion. The hope is that, through these ideas, they might be integrated into what makes us 'one body' even before they come to formally share in the bread and wine. This is about learning, as Jerome Berryman puts it, the 'second language' of the Christian family[5]. If we really believe that children are not just the future of the church but are part of the 'now' of the church and that they truly belong, then we can't underestimate the power of including them in one of our most fundamental rites.

5. Jerome Berryman, *The Spiritual Guidance of Children: Montessori, Godly Play and the Future,* (New York, Morehouse Publishing, 2013), page 3.

   23

Experimenting with symbols, role play and participation

It's fascinating to chat to those who work with under 5s and to discover that, across the country and, indeed, across the world, many churches are already experimenting in this area, seeking to draw their youngest children playfully and reverently into experiencing Communion in their own way. The next chapter gives a flavour of many ways in which under 5s are being encouraged to share in the story of this special meal and here we will take a snapshot look at a few of those stories.

One incredible example of how children can be drawn into participation in a meaningful way is the Nursery Rhyme Mass, written by Father Simon Rundell, with a text generously available under Creative Commons Licence, so that as many churches as possible can share in the liturgy and celebration. Based on the Church of England liturgy, all prayers are set to well-known nursery rhyme tunes and sung as the service progresses. A simple confession is sung to the tune of 'Twinkle, twinkle, little star'; an acknowledgement of forgiveness is sung to 'If you're happy and you know it', and this wonderful invitation to Communion is sung to the tune of 'Three blind mice':

> Come and eat, come and drink,
> you're welcome here, come quite near,
> share in his body and blood with us,
> it tastes like wine and bread but just
> know that inside it's not quite thus
> share the food of God.[6]
>
> (Father Simon Rundell, reproduced with permission and
> under Creative Commons Licence from
> http://www.nurseryrhymemass.org.uk/texts/)

A growing number of churches are engaging with this material and exploring how such services can incorporate young children and their families into the story of Communion. Here is one such story:

6. http://www.nurseryrhymemass.org.uk/texts/

24

Case Study: Nursery Rhyme Mass, Kilternan Parish, Dublin, Ireland

The Church of Ireland minister, Revd Rob Clements, has been in post for about a year and has been experimenting with using the Nursery Rhyme Mass as a regular all-age alternative to the traditional Eucharistic service. While Rob's congregation doesn't sing the entire service, key parts of the liturgy, including gathering, confession and absolution, creed, prayers and sending out, follow the nursery rhyme settings written by Fr Simon.

For Rob, the Nursery Rhyme Mass is part of a concerted effort to help the families of his congregation to understand what it means to worship together. With this service, he is able to let parents know that it's ok for their child 'to be' without the need for shushing. Children from the youngest age are able to feel 'I belong here'.

Children are included as much as possible in the service and come up to the communion rail as the elements are being prepared, so that they can see exactly what is happening. It is still early days in their experimentation with this service, but Rob would like, in the future to include the children in the setting of the table; helping to pour and fold so that they understand more fully their involvement in the community meal of God's family. He would also love to encourage a different family each time to bake bread together and then bring it to be broken, again establishing the image of the family meal.

For Rob, age is not a barrier for those who come to the mystery of Communion. As children at school are increasingly encouraged to learn by participation and 'doing', Rob is convinced that the best way to learn about the table and God's hospitality is to come to the table. He speaks of the difference he sees in how both children and parents approach Communion through this service. Where, in the past, children might have been left in the pews when their parents came forward to receive, now the children come to the rail and there is delight on the parents' faces when they see their children actively involved.

Churches elsewhere are looking to the use of play and symbols as they try to include under 5s into the story of this special meal. An especially interesting resource in this respect is the 'liturgy box' inspired by Betty Pedley and developed by Carolynn Pritchard, an adminstrator of the Spiritual Child Network.[7] A box (possibly a shoe box or similar size) is filled with symbolic items correlating to different parts of the Communion liturgy and children are encouraged to interact with these items as the service progresses. Items might include connecting toys such as 'Octons' to illustrate the 'gathering' aspect of the service; a cross to be held during the confession and wooden egg cups and small plates to help children act out using a chalice and paten. These symbol-filled boxes are particularly useful to help children and families engage with the elements of a Communion service where there is no formal provision for children, and the concept behind them, as we will see, has enormous potential to be expanded as an interactive experience for the whole congregation. Liturgy boxes have also provided a jumping-off point for the story below, in which a box of Communion-themed objects has led to some significant role playing amongst children under 5.

Case Study: Communion Treasure Box, St Helen's, Selston

In our church most of the primary school age children have been prepared to receive Communion and so have some knowledge and understanding of what is happening during the service and when they come forward to receive the bread and wine. We were looking for a way to include the younger children in what was happening so, for the last year, we have been experimenting with a 'Communion treasure box'.

The treasure box is loosely based around the contents of the 'liturgy boxes' that we first came across on the Spiritual Child Network website and holds symbols relevant to different aspects of what is happening in the service. Our vicar found an old coal box in a charity shop that looks very much like a treasure chest and that worked really well because we wanted to create a sense of what was inside the chest being 'special' or like treasure.

7. http://www.spiritualchild.co.uk/liturgyboxes.html

Inside the box we put a selection of signs and symbols that we hoped would be easy to play with but also relevant to different parts of what was going on in the service:

- Handkerchiefs in the four liturgical colours (red, white, purple and green) plus a couple of extra white ones as 'purificators'.
- Wooden crosses and doves
- Metal cups and plates (found for bargain prices in a charity shop)
- Wooden bread
- Wooden and fabric hearts (as a symbol of God's love)
- Battery-operated tea lights
- 'Globe' bouncy balls (as a reminder of God as Creator)

On the first Sunday after we'd made it, we put the box at the front of church and waited to see what the children would do. It was fascinating! Two of our under 5s investigated what was inside and immediately picked up the cups and white handkerchiefs. They gave each other 'sips' from the cups and, completely unprompted, wiped them with the cloths as they had seen the chalice assistants doing at the front. They then went off to repeat the process with their parents!

Seeing the children role playing with 'Communion cups' illustrates so clearly the fact that our children are absorbing the language and rituals of the church community from an early age. When they play, they are making sense of the story they hear and see being presented from the front, but they are also entering into a much deeper understanding of what is happening than we might at first imagine. This is the most wonderful discovery of our work amongst under 5s. We should never underestimate their capacity to connect on the deepest level.

While liturgy boxes are an amazing resource to help children to play around the themes and symbols of Holy Communion, Carolynn has developed the sense of liturgical play even further and is exploring the integration of children and their carers at every level of the Communion service. Here is her story of a very special service which has emerged in her Cambridge church:

Case Study: Carolynn Pritchard, The Ark, Michaelhouse Chapel, Cambridge

'The Ark' is a weekly Church of England service of Holy Communion for carers, babies and preschool children at Michaelhouse Chapel Cambridge. The aim is that children are incorporated into the worship through 'liturgical play'. The worship space is set with liturgical play materials which reflect the colour and season of the church year, sacraments, different elements of the liturgy and the Gospel reading.

The service starts with the children ringing small hand bells and lighting the high altar candles. We then sing and sign 'Jesus' love is very wonderful' or 'He's got the whole world in his hands'. This is followed by a sung Kyrie Confession with everyone holding a wooden cross and then the Peruvian Gloria with ribbon rings and miniature maracas; even the tiniest babies can participate. The children learn the pattern of the liturgy and often hand the baskets of items round of their own volition. A simplified Gospel reading follows which is then re-told for the children using pictures, figures and objects in a Godly Play style. We then wonder about the story together. During the prayers the children choose prayer pictures on the themes of church, world, sickness and remembrance, and suggest people and topics for prayer. Between the prayers we sign and sign 'O Lord, hear our prayer'. Everyone shares the peace, and babies learn to offer a hand even before they can speak. Children of all ages join in the offertory and help laying the low Communion table, carrying the chalice, paten, jugs, bread and linens, spreading the corporal, pouring the wine and water and washing the priest's fingers. During the offertory we sing 'We bring this bread . . . We bring this wine' to the Taizé Magnificat tune. Children will gather around the Communion table during the Eucharistic Prayer. They often watch intently and play with miniature chalices, patens, jugs, bread and grapes, imitating the gestures, repeating words and sharing play elements; they are engaged in active participation in the Eucharist. We have Bishop's dispensation to communicate baptised children with

   28

the bread if the parents so wish. The service ends with a continuation of the offertory hymn, 'Blessed be God', followed by the Blessing and Dismissal. The service ends with ribbons and shakers and singing the 'African Alleluia'. The children then ring bells and blow out candles, signalling the end of the service.

The children are learning the ritual, symbols and rhythms of the liturgy through the liturgical play, even before they can talk, and by the time they leave us they have a significant knowledge and symbolic understanding of the Communion service. The rich liturgical and symbolic landscape of 'The Ark' has been transformational in the children's liturgical formation and exemplifies the understanding that when children are incorporated into the worshipping community they are 'appropriate liturgical participants even in infancy'[8].

As we have seen, even the youngest children can communicate a sense of the mystery and importance of what is happening around them. As the following story illustrates, even those children who are not used to the language and rituals of church, are able to understand deeply the significance and 'holiness' of participating in the Communion story.

Case Study:
Revd Dr Helen Hooley, Methodist Minister

I was invited to talk to the nursery class in my local primary school (not a church school, but the head is a Christian). Their theme was 'senses'.

I took a number of items from chapel: the wooden font (about two feet high – touch and see), the velvet pulpit hanging (touch), a Lion Graphic Bible (see), anointing oil (smell),

8. Louis Weil, *Children and Worship* in D. Apostolos-Cappadona (Ed.), *The Sacred Play of Children*, (New York: Seabury Press,1983), page 55.

bread (taste), grape juice and individual communion cups (taste), a CD of 'Our God is a great big God' (hear).

I spoke about the different ways we experience God. I put some oil on the wrists of each child and we talked about how the whole room now smelled nice. I passed around all the objects for them to touch and look at and share with their neighbour. Then I spoke about bread and wine (they knew something about it representing Jesus' body and blood) and I gave each of them a piece of bread and a drink of juice (not a Communion service though!). We ended by singing the song with actions.

The children were really engaged with this. I understood that something important had happened. They were all very reverent, if I can use that word; they seemed to understand that these things were really special. It felt a very calm space, particularly after using the oil. They seemed to treat it as if they had been given a very special present, like holding a baby chick very gently. They were surprised that they were allowed to have some bread and juice, that being allowed to join in and do something, not just be expected to sit and listen and look, made them feel part of something bigger.

The children in Helen's story were able to feel part of 'something bigger' when they took the bread and juice. Helen, an adult, acted as a facilitator in bringing them to a sense of their part in a bigger community of faith. It is especially exciting, however, when that scenario is turned completely on its head and our children themselves become the facilitators. It is often through the role play of the youngest children that adults themselves are challenged to see new things. Given the freedom to respond and explore creatively, children have the capacity to teach adults about the story we share.

Case Study: Revd Amanda Lees, St John's College, Bramcote

From aged 4, my younger son would join in the celebration of Communion at my theological training college.

All young children, many of preschool age, were invited to gather around a very low level Communion table and sit on the floor along with the celebrant. The children were invited to hold the chalice while the president blessed the elements and recounted the passion narrative. This included a chalice of non-alcoholic wine also.

My son relished such services – they were at the centre of a table of invitation, yet the rituals they observed and the liturgy they participated in were not 'dialled down'. From such exposure, my younger son would regularly take his bread and squash when we were enjoying a family meal and re-enact the breaking of bread and giving of wine, reciting the words, 'This is my body . . . This is my blood.' After a while, my older children would then join in with the words and before we knew it, we were all remembering what Jesus had done for us – at all times and in all places! My son had made and understood a deep connection for us between our daily family meal and the love and fellowship of the church family of God.

In the following chapters we will get a glimpse of how our under 5s can explore and express their part in the story of Communion through play and creativity. There will be practical ideas for age-related groups outside of the service and also for those children who stay in the service. We will look at the role of parents and other adults in facilitating that exploration and we will hear more stories from practitioners – not only of how they are helping children to encounter Communion but also of how the children, themselves, are teaching adults about what it means to be part of the body of Christ sharing this special meal.

 **Useful books:**

- **Children at Communion: How to Include Children in the Eucharist**
  Trevor Lloyd, (Cambridge: Grove Books, 2010).

- **Infants and Children, Baptism and Communion**
  Peter Reiss, (Cambridge: Grove Books, 2015).

 Useful websites:

- **Nursery Rhyme Mass**: http://www.nurseryrhymemass.org.uk/texts/
- **Spiritual Child Network:**
  http://www.spiritualchild.co.uk/liturgyboxes.html
- **Flame Creative Kids:**
  http://flamecreativekids.blogspot.co.uk/p/exploring-holy-communion.html

Chapter 3

More Stories of Under 5s Connecting with Worship and Communion

In putting this book together, I have been overwhelmed by the encouraging stories of churches, ministers and families across the world who have been exploring and experiencing the many ways in which our under 5s connect with worship and with Holy Communion. Here is a small sample of the real stories people have contributed. Be inspired!

 ## Revd Traci Smith

I love to tell the story of how we ended up at church one time thinking there was to be a lunch before the service (it was scheduled for after the service) and my children came to worship ravenous. When the elements were distributed, my son Clayton said 'THAT IS NOT ENOUGH FOOD'. I always thought it was a sort of theological statement.

 ## Revd Andy Stinson

St Bartholomew's Church is a small village church near Chester. We run our Pram Service once every half term. It is a service aimed at children aged 0-4 and is attended by the village's preschool as well as individual children and their carers.

The service uses a regular 'liturgy' of songs and prayers as we gather, welcome, confess, praise and introduce the story for that service. The repeated elements of the service allow children who can't read to engage with and join in with the service and we will often explore the story through play, song and craft to reinforce the message.

   35

The simple repeated elements allow the children to take the first steps in developing their faith as we engage with God in a service they thoroughly enjoy. The children hear that God loves them, welcomes them, forgives them and cares for them. They learn stories about Jesus and simple theological concepts, for example 'Jesus died to take away the bad things'.

Watching the children engage with the service and grow in confidence to join in, allows the children to learn what it is to worship and helps them take the first steps in growing their own faith.

Revd Sharon Lord

There is a 3-year-old at our church, who likes to stand next to me when I announce the peace and when I say the blessing. He is quite a handful normally, but during those moments he stands completely still, as if he realises the significance of it all. We have accepted children into Holy Communion, so he receives the bread with as much reverence as the adults. His language is delayed so he doesn't verbally express much.

Revd Anna Alls

My children always attended church with us and always came up to the communion rail for a blessing while we received Communion. I remember going into the girls' bedroom one day and seeing they'd lined up their dolls and teddies, each was working their way down the row with a plate and a cup. We'd never had a proper discussion about Communion but they'd seen it done and enjoyed enacting. I guess the little one was only 2. I remember the togetherness of their game, as much as the symbolism of their actions

Olivia A. J. Haines

Our little girl loves clapping along with the songs and hymns, and sometimes uses her tambourine. She can't say the words, but it doesn't mean she isn't worshipping. Recently, she has started holding her hand out to people during the peace. It isn't something we've purposefully done, she just wants to be a part of it. Similarly, when we approach the altar she stands on her own and holds her hand out for a wafer. She wants to do what the adults are doing, and why not? Our vicar is more than happy for her to have the bread, she is baptised after all. We look forward to having the conversation about what it means as she grows up.

Vicki Evans

I had one child who regularly participated in Holy Communion in the Uniting Church. We attended an Anglican church and she was refused Communion because she was 4. At the end of the service while being greeted by the minister at the door, she told the minister that she was part of ALL, she had said all the prayers with everyone else and she understood that Jesus welcomes ALL and she was remembering his death and resurrection just like everyone else until he comes again. The minister said that any time she comes back she is welcome to take Communion with the rest of the adults.

Marie-Pierre Tonnon-Louant

In our church (in Belgium), all children are welcome at the Holy Supper, as long as the parents agree with the idea. Children aged 3 and 4 come, always respectfully. They are the sign of abundance and generosity. We share bread. There are always big and little pieces on the plate; the 3 and 4-year-olds spontaneously take the big pieces. They are respectful but they don't need to be polite. They see a big piece of bread and they take it. And as long as there is enough bread for everybody, we enjoy that they do it because it is a sign of grace: not a polite system, not catechism and reason: just abundance (abondance).

Revd Jemma Allen

I was doing Communion preparation with two preschoolers. After looking at the Communion stories in their Bibles, we got out the home Communion set to look at all the pieces. I told the boys that when someone gave them bread to eat, they would say 'the body of Christ' and the cup was shared with 'the blood of Christ'. We talked about bodies and blood and the boys talked about bodies being how you are in a place (presence, in adult language) and blood is what keeps you alive (if all your blood comes out you die). Presence and life seemed a pretty good theology of Eucharist to me. I'm a priest in the Anglican Church in Aotearoa, New Zealand and Polynesia. In our province baptism is the only prerequisite to Communion, but we also do ongoing Communion education, which some parents prefer their children to wait for.

 Revd Ally Barrett

My son: 'You said that the wine was a visible sign, but I think the really important thing isn't what the wine looks like, it's how it feels. You drink the wine and it's warm as it goes down, like a hug – so it's the wine being warm that's a sacrament of God's love.'

 Alex Sanderson

At our church baptised children (baptised as infants, not yet confirmed) can be given some of the bread by parents or Godparents. I love that, because we made those promises, we can bring them to the table and include them. My then 4-year-old wanted to take part and we were debating this and wondering if it was the right time for her, so in the end we asked her what she thought it was all about. She was very clear: 'The bread makes us remember Jesus!'

 Revd Karen Ware-Jackson

I haven't done anything specifically geared towards the 0-4 crowd beyond welcoming them to the table. I have baked the bread for Communion with my own kids, which is very neat and I let the kids take the leftover bread (and now the juice as well) to their table in the pray ground and they finish it off in the service. They all LOVE the 'Jesus bread' because we typically use Hawaiian bread or homemade challah, so it's slightly sweet. I also tell everyone to feel free to take a big hunk of bread (we do intinction) but the kids are the only ones who take me up on it. They always take great big pieces. I love that. I'm Presbyterian Church USA, so we tend to be a bit more 'low church' than C of E or ECUSA.

Chapter 4

Three practical Sessions for children aged 0-2 in a church crèche Setting

The following sessions are written to be used in church 'crèche' style settings. This might be a place where younger children are supervised during a church service or in an area where parents sit with their children during the service. The sessions pick up on key themes that play a part in the story of Holy Communion and use a selection of toys and activities to explore them. In all of this exploration, the most important thing is that the children feel welcome, safe and cared for as part of the church family. Secondary to that is the potential for the children to play around the themes, experience awe and wonder moments and create their own meaning from the resources provided. Have fun!

NOTES:

Each session outline provides a series of ideas that can be used, including possible toys to use, stories and songs that might be helpful and 'treasure basket' and 'heuristic play' ideas.

o By no means do you have to use all of the ideas! Just use one or two of the sections or choose a few of the ideas to mix in amongst the other toys you generally use and it will help to tie the theme together.

o Have a short time where you stop play and gather the children together to share a snack, sing, tell a story or play a game. This is a way of helping to draw out the theme of the session.

○ Be ready to be amazed at what the children come up with as they explore and play.

○ 'Treasure baskets' are usually baskets filled with a variety of natural or household objects: metal, wood, shell, leather, fabric etc. They are really good for babies who can sit, but not yet crawl, and the idea is that the children can independently explore the items in the basket with all their senses. With this in mind, always be sure to use things that are safe for babies to put in their mouths!

○ 'Heuristic play' involves collections of everyday items which more mobile children can play with in a very open-ended way. Instead of intervening or directing, it's better if adults just sit back and watch the amazing things the children come up with as they play! Children in the 3-5s range will also enjoy heuristic play so, if you have a crèche group that involves children who are older than 2, this is a good option.

SESSION 1

Theme: Gathering/Family

So that the idea of being part of God's big family when we come together at church can be explored, suggestions for this session are centred around the idea of family, community and connecting. For the very youngest, the treasure basket contains items that are soft and smooth, to help establish a sense of comfort and reassurance. The suggested story is a retelling of Psalm 139, establishing the idea of God being a comforting, fatherly presence who is always with us. The song draws together themes from all three sessions.

Toys

- Family photos in plastic frames
- Mega Blocks or Duplo®
- Connecting toys
- 'Family' dolls
- Doll's houses

Treasure Basket

(Theme of comfort, softness, warmth and reassurance)
- Lengths of ribbon
- Piece of velvet
- Knitted square
- Felt square

- Wooden blocks

- Wooden pastry brush (very soft bristles!)
- Wooden cross
- Small teddy bear

Story/Song/Time together

(To the tune of 'Twinkle, twinkle, little star')

We are a family,

Jesus here with you and me.

You love us, Jesus, and you give

food we need for us to live.

Help us go and love our friends

just as you love us. Amen

Always near Me by Susie Poole

Heuristic Play:

- Napkin rings or shower curtain rings
- Mug trees
- Ribbons
- Peg people / dolly pegs

Craft Idea

Make hand prints and draw faces on the fingers to make 'families'.

SESSION 2

Theme: Special meals

In order to explore the 'special meal' aspect of Communion, the ideas for this session are very much based around food and sharing food – both play and real. The suggested stories are a retelling of the feeding of the 5000 and a version of the Easter story, which will include the story of the Last Supper. As before, the song draws on all three themes for these sessions.

Toys

- Play food (particularly bread!)
- Play kitchen (if you have one!)
- Picnic mat
- Plastic plates, cups, knives, forks, spoons

Treasure Basket (food theme)

- Orange (the texture of the peel is great!)
- Lemon
- Wooden or metal egg cup
- Wooden spoon

- Basket of oranges / lemons / apples (let the children explore the textures of the skins)
- Play dough and cookie cutters
- Books about food

- Felt 'bread'
- Small wooden or metal bowl
- Metal whisk
- Metal tea strainer
- Wooden cross

Story/Song/Time Together

(To the tune of 'Twinkle, twinkle, little star')

We are a family,
Jesus here with you and me.
You love us, Jesus, and you give
food we need for us to live.
Help us go and love our friends
just as you love us. Amen

Jesus Feeds a Crowd
by Maggie Barfield

The Easter Story by Juliet David

Heuristic Play

- Corks
- Bun tins
- Wooden or plastic hearts
- Egg boxes
- Tins
- Small boxes

Craft Idea

Work with children to spread butter or substitute on bread and then spread on some jam or sprinkle on some sugar strands. Eat the bread together.

SESSION 3

Theme: Gifts/Going out

This theme helps to reflect what happens at the end of Communion where we are sent out into the world to share Jesus' love. Ideas centre around journeys, outdoor clothing and 'gifts', reflecting the gift of love we are sent to share. The suggested book is a retelling of some New Testament stories, which will reflect the love that Jesus gave to other people.

   44

Toys

- Dressing up:
  - Coats
  - Shoes
  - Wellingtons
  - Hats
  - Gloves
  - Scarves
- Bags, suitcase
- Toy cars and road play mats
- Wind-up toys
- Books about cars and other transport

Treasure Basket

(special/ shiny theme)

- Fabric hearts
- Ribbons
- CD
- Hand bells
- Small mirrors
- Small metal tin with lid
- Piece of velvet
- Wooden cross

Story/Song/Time Together

(To the tune of 'Twinkle, twinkle, little star')

We are a family,
Jesus here with you and me.
You love us, Jesus, and you give
food we need for us to live.
Help us go and love our friends
just as you love us. Amen

The Little Bible Storybook
by Maggie Barfield

Heuristic Play

- Dolly pegs/ peg people
- Gift boxes
- Gift bags
- Ribbons

Craft idea

Dip toy car wheels in paint and let children roll them across paper to create painted 'journeys'.

   45

Useful books:

- **Always near Me**
  Susie Poole (B&H Publishing Group, 2014).

- **Jesus Feeds a Crowd**
  Maggie Barfield (Scripture Union, 2012).

- **The Easter Story**
  Juliet David (Candle Books, 2012).

- **The Little Bible Storybook**
  Maggie Barfield (Scripture Union, 2007).

Useful websites:

- **For treasure baskets and heuristic play ideas:**

  http://www.communityplaythings.co.uk

  http://www.nurseryworld.co.uk/treasure-baskets-heuristic-play

- **Christian play-based ideas:**

  http://allplayonsunday.blogspot.co.uk

Chapter

5

Four practical Sessions for children aged 3-5 within a Junior church Setting

Here are four sessions to help you explore some of the themes connected with Holy Communion in a more formal setting e.g. junior church or Sunday school. Again, these are all suggestions and by no means feel you have to do everything!

The most important aspect of these sessions is the time when you can chat to the children about what they are thinking, so the 'play' and 'craft' suggestions are deliberately free and open-ended. The idea is that children will have the chance to explore and question and that adults will be facilitators of this.

Each session has a Take home sheet. This is an activity that parents can do at home to continue the theme and discussion.

Suggested activities in bold type and underlined will need preparation before the session and further details can be found at the end of the chapter (with the exception of the Communion box, which you will find details of in chapter 6).

SESSION 1

Theme: Remembering

It might be useful to have made a **'memory' box** of items you can show to the children. The items inside the box should remind you of people or events in your life e.g. photos, tickets, items people have given you.

Story: The Last Supper

Read and act out using bread and juice.

Things to talk about:

- Think about the link between the story and what the children have seen happening in Holy Communion.

- What does 'remember' mean?

49

- What do you remember doing when you were at home this morning?
- Why do we remember Jesus?
- Show children your memory box and talk about the things inside it.

Game: Remembering tray game.

Put items on a tray, then cover it and remove one. Take the cover off and get children to try and remember what is missing.

Craft: Use card or foam sheets cut into 'people' shapes. Get children to decorate them so that the card person reminds them of someone they love e.g. a parent or a friend. Talk about what they have done to remind them of that person e.g. colours they have used for hair or clothes.

Choice/Play:

Make **scented play dough** (see How to sheets, page 87) and ask children what the smell reminds them of as they play with it.

Play with cups, plates, hankies, play bread.

Role play cafés or kitchens.

Prayer:

Talk about your memory box. What would the children put inside their own memory box? Ask children to draw it on a slip of paper and put the pieces into a 'special' box. Thank God for those memories.

Take home:

Give each child a box (e.g. a plastic sandwich box) and ask them to make a memory box at home. (See Take home sheet 1, page 85.)

Song

(To the tune of 'Twinkle, twinkle, little star')

We are a family,
Jesus here with you and me.
You love us, Jesus, and you give
food we need for us to live.
Help us go and love our friends
just as you love us. Amen

SESSION 2

Theme: A Special Meal

Story: The Last Supper

Read a different version of the story from the one you read last week and see what the children remember.

Remind the children about the 'remembering' theme from last week and talk about how Jesus was a special person, so we have a special meal to remember him.

- What would you have for a special meal?

- What else would you do to make the meal special?

- Talk about the bread and the wine we use for Jesus' special meal and why they are important.

- What else have the children observed about Communion that makes it seem special? They might talk about the white cloth, the special cup or a whole range of things!

Game: Taste test

Blindfold a child and see if they can guess a food you give them to taste. Let all the children have a turn with a different food. Beware of allergies!

Craft: Use collage materials to make a 'special meal' of favourite food (stick onto paper plates).

or

If you have access to an oven, buy some bread mix or chilled bread dough and help the children to make their own special bread that can then be cooked and eaten.

Choice/Play

Remember me play dough mat

Tablecloths, plastic plates, cutlery, cups

Setting table role play

Play food

Colouring Sheet: A special meal

Prayer

Before the session, cut out some pictures of different foods and drinks from magazines and shop adverts.

Get each child to choose one of the pictures and say 'thank you' to God for that thing.

Take Home

Recipe for simple scones that can be made at home.
(See Take home sheet 2, page 85.)

Song

(To the tune of 'Twinkle, twinkle, little star')

We are a family,
Jesus here with you and me.
You love us, Jesus, and you give
food we need for us to live.
Help us go and love our friends
just as you love us. Amen

SESSION 3

Theme: Belonging to God's family

Before you start this session, it would be useful to have made a **'Communion box'** of items to explore.

Explain:

Show the cups and the bread from the Communion box.

Last time, we learned the story of the Last Supper, where Jesus asked his disciples to have bread and wine to remember him. We remember Jesus because he is very special to us and we want to show that we are part of his team – we belong together. Sharing a meal like Communion is a symbol of us being a big family.

- What is a family?
- Who is in your family?
- What does it feel like to be part of a family?

Look at the symbols in the Communion box and discuss with the children what they mean and/or how they are used.

Game:

Work as a team to use plastic cups or plastic bricks to build a tower. The team with the tallest tower at the end of the time limit is the winner.

Think about what it is like to be part of a team, cheering each other on and helping each other.

Craft:

Make body of Christ crayons
(See How to sheets, page 87.)

All of the different crayon parts are melted together to make one piece. Lots of different people come together in church and when we take Communion because we are all part of God's family.

Choice/Play

- **Colouring Sheet: I am part of God's big family**
- Play with dolls/ peg figures.
- Role play homes and families.
- Play with the items in the Communion box.
- Play the **Communion symbols matching game**.

Prayer:

Thank God for people who are friends or who are in our families. Write about them or draw them on people shapes and hang them on a prayer tree.

Take home

God's big family play dough mat

(See Take home sheet 3, page 86.)

Song

(To the tune of 'Twinkle, twinkle, little star')

We are a family,
Jesus here with you and me.
You love us, Jesus, and you give
food we need for us to live.
Help us go and love our friends
just as you love us. Amen

SESSION 4

Theme: Sharing God's love

Recap:

Remind children about the previous two weeks' sessions.

Holy Communion helps us to remember Jesus.

It reminds us that we are part of God's big family.

Explain that because Jesus loves us, he wants us to go out and show love to other people too.

- What is love?

- How do you show someone that you love them?

- What does love feel like?

Game:

Communion symbols matching game.

Play the game in a big group or in smaller groups with an adult.

Match the symbols on the cards to items in your Communion box and talk about how they relate to Holy Communion.

Craft:

Decorate card or foam hearts to give to someone they love. Use sequins, glitter, coloured pens, collage scraps, buttons or anything that the children like to use.

- Talk to children about who they are going to give their heart to and why.

- Could they show this person they love them in other ways too?

Choice/Play:

- Communion box items
- **<u>Colouring Sheet:</u>**
  <u>Sharing God's love with others</u>
- Play dough with 'people' and 'heart' shaped cutters.
- Symbols matching game.
- Doll/peg doll family role play.

Prayer:

Use a heart-shaped cutter to cut hearts from slices of bread.

Give children a bread heart each. Ask God to help us to show love to others and then eat the bread together.

Take home

Spreading Heart Prayers

(See Take home sheet 4, page 86.)

Song

(To the tune of 'Twinkle, twinkle, little star')

We are a family,
Jesus here with you and me.
You love us, Jesus, and you give
food we need for us to live.
Help us go and love our friends
just as you love us. Amen

The following sheets can be found in Chapter 8: Downloadable resources

- Remember me play dough mat
- God's big family play dough mat
- Colouring sheet: I am part of God's big family
- Colouring sheet: Sharing God's love with others
- Colouring sheet: A special meal
- Communion symbols matching game
- Take home sheets
- How to sheets

Information on how to make a 'Communion box' can be found in the next chapter.

Chapter 6

Using resources during a Communion Service

While the previous two chapters have looked at how children might be introduced to the story and themes of Holy Communion in more formal 'junior church' style sessions, this chapter will focus on participation and inclusion in the service itself. This is especially useful for times when there are no children's groups available.

Each of the ideas below can be used in 'pray-ground' or children's area which should ideally be close to the front of the church, so that children can see the visuals associated with the liturgy or Communion story and can feel more a part of the church family. Depending on your church set up, this might not always be possible but it really seems to make a difference if the children are closer to the action – not just for the children themselves, but also to help the adults see that the children are part of the story too.

As always, you certainly don't need to use all of these suggestions. Choose which you think would work best in your context and have a go at rotating ideas! In our church we usually choose three or four activities per service.

 ## Communion box or treasure chest

Based on the Liturgy boxes explored in chapter 2, this is a collection of symbolic and role play items that will help children to explore and experiment with the themes and story of Communion. What you choose to put in the box will depend very much on the tradition of your church and what you use to administer Communion. Feel free to mix and match. Put the items into a big box and let the children take the lead!

Suggested items to choose from for the box:

- Handkerchiefs in liturgical colours (if this is your tradition)

- White handkerchiefs as purificators (to wipe the cup with)

    59

- Hearts (to symbolise God's love)
- Globe balls (to symbolise God as creator and his love for the world)
- Crosses
- Doves
- Battery-operated candles
- Cups/ goblets
- Plates
- Children's Bibles or Bible story books
- Play 'people'
- Kaleidoscopes (there is a lot of awe and wonder involved in using a kaleidoscope!)
- Play bread
- Play grapes
- Duplo® (to symbolise 'gathering' or joining together as a family)

 Play dough mats

Play dough mats are a real favourite and help children to engage with some of the themes of Communion in a very tactile way. The idea with play dough mats is to print them off and then laminate them. This way they can be used multiple times and it is much easier to clean the play dough off when the children have finished. The play dough mats suggested for use here are 'Remember me' and 'God's big family'. 'Remember me' looks at the theme of special meals and 'God's big family' looks at the theme of belonging. When we have used these in our church, we generally set out three or four on a table as one of several options for children to explore during the service.

Colouring sheets

Like play dough mats, the colouring sheets are very popular. While children at this age might not necessarily connect with the words, they often do connect

with the imagery relating to what is happening in the service. The colouring sheets suggested here and available to download, (see chapter 8) are:

- A special meal
- I am part of God's big family
- Sharing God's love with others

Worship materials

A lot of young children (and adults) like the chance to be up and active during times of worship, so it's a great idea to have a selection of things to help them to participate.

- Shakers and other percussion instruments
- Flags for dancing or waving
- Ribbons or streamers
- Items to inspire awe and wonder: e.g. kaleidoscopes, reflection bottles (see below), bubbles
- Creative items e.g. chalk and chalk boards, fuzzy felt (see below)

Reflection bottles

These are so simple to make and yet so mesmerising to use! They really inspire a sense of awe and wonder but also allow space to be still and reflect.

You will need: a bottle of water with a lid (an average 500ml bottle is perfect but bigger bottles are good too!), all-purpose glue or super glue, glitter, food colouring, vegetable oil.

Type 1: Glitter and water

- Fill the bottle with water and add two tablespoons of glitter to it. It looks great if you use two different colours (one tablespoon of each).

- Put some glue around the top of the bottle and screw the lid on. Let the glue set so that the bottle can't be opened.

- Shake the bottle and watch as the glitter swirls and settles.

Type 2: Oil and water

- Fill two thirds of the bottle with water. Add food colouring to colour the water. Use vegetable or baby oil to fill the remaining third of the bottle.

- Put some glue around the top of the bottle and screw the lid on. Let the glue set so that the bottle can't be opened.

- Shake the bottle and watch the oil and water mix and then separate.

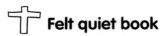 Felt quiet book

I made a quiet book for the 0-2s in the congregation but found that some of the older ladies couldn't put it down! This item is called a 'quiet book' because it is made of felt, so doesn't make a lot of noise when it is used, but this is not a reflection on how children should be in the service!

The best way to explain the quiet book is to share pictures of it and these can be found at **http://flamecreativekids.blogspot.co.uk/2016/09/church-felt-quiet-book-for-babies-my.html** Basically, each page is made of a square of felt onto which has been sewn or glued a picture or interactive activity. Pages are very tactile and generally include a range of textures. The felt book I created included pictures and activities based around the themes of church and Communion symbols.

- **Front Cover**: A cross and 4 flaps to lift, revealing a dove, a heart, a church and a Bible (foam stickers).

- **Page 1**: 'Welcome': 5 people shapes in different colours, attached to the page with ribbon.

- **Page 2**: 'Light': 3 candle shapes. Flames are hidden under flaps.

- **Page 3**: 'Love': A heart with a zip through the middle. Open the heart to reveal some people shapes stuck to a ribbon that can be pulled out.

- **Page 4**: 'Cross': A picture of a cross with an identical picture cut into jigsaw pieces. The jigsaw pieces can be matched and velcroed on top of the original picture. Each piece is attached to the page with a ribbon so the pieces won't be lost.

- **Page 5**: 'Communion': A felt cup and piece of bread. Lift the flaps to reveal red wine in the cup and bread inside the darker crust.

- **Page 6**: 'Rainbow': Match the button to the correct colour stripe in the rainbow. Buttons are attached to the page by ribbon, so can't be lost and the button can be velcroed into place on the stripe.

- **Page 7**: 'Spirit': A dove with feather tail and velcro body.

- **Page 8**: 'Water': A felt jar with blue and white ribbons of water pouring out of the top. For added texture, blue and white buttons have been sewn onto the ribbons.

 ## Fuzzy felt

This activity is really easy to make but provides so much scope for creative involvement. Cut large cross shapes out of pieces of felt and then cut a collection of other, smaller shapes and shards. Give the children free reign to decorate the crosses with the smaller felt pieces.

 ## Prayer cubes

Intercession and prayer is an integral part of most church services, including Holy Communion. These cubes are a fun way of introducing topics of prayer to younger children and encouraging them to join in with praying. Print off and make up the cube. Throw the cube and pray the type of prayer that lands face up. With children under 5, I tend to focus on 'please', 'sorry' and 'thank you' prayers. The prayer cube is in the downloadable resources in chapter 8.

 ## Invitations to play

An 'Invitation to play' is an arrangement of materials or resources that will encourage children to explore and play in an open-ended way. The adult intentionally sets up the 'invitation' but what the children do with it is up to them.

Some of the resources mentioned above lend themselves very naturally to invitations to play, so here are some ideas to help draw out the themes of Communion.

   63

Set up the invitation to play on a table and see what happens during the service!

- Cups, plates, play bread, handkerchiefs
- Play dough, plastic or wooden hearts and wooden people figures
- Fuzzy felt crosses
- Duplo® or wooden blocks and peg dolls or 'people figures'
- Hearts, gift boxes and small crosses
- Play dough, plates, cups and Duplo®
- Small crosses, black paper or card and coloured chalk
- Crosses, hearts and pipe cleaners

 Play churches

Another brilliant way to help children to role play and explore what they see happening is to get hold of a 'play church'. There are wooden, plastic and even fabric churches on the market that come complete with church furniture and characters to interact with. It has been fascinating to observe children move from playing with the play church to role play, in which they themselves take on the actions and act out the rituals.

 Useful links for resources:

- **For Communion box, Play dough mats, Colouring sheets, Reflection bottles, Felt quiet book, and Fuzzy felt**: search at http://flamecreativekids.blogspot.co.uk

- **Liturgy boxes**: http://www.spiritualchild.co.uk/liturgyboxes.html

- **Invitations to play**: http://www.bdeducation.org.uk/children/under-5s/online-resources

- **Play churches**: http://www.tts-group.co.uk/soft-play-fabric-church/1003550.html
  http://www.articlesoffaith.co.uk/soft-church-1.html
  http://www.articlesoffaith.co.uk/place-of-worship-church.html

Chapter 7

The role of adults, mealtime rituals and Celebrations in the hOMe

If we truly believe that children are equal members of God's family and that they have immense potential to worship and to connect with the story of Holy Communion, then we have a responsibility, as adults, to help them do so. We must be facilitators and tool sharers. Our aim must not be to dictate play, pushing towards an 'objective' but to be a partner with the children, exploring the richness of symbols and actions together with them, while remaining aware and respectful of the child's own intrinsic ability to respond to God. We are there with them, alongside them, observing and cheering them on as they make the journey of faith. We cannot leave this journey at the church door and wait for it to be picked up at the same time next week. The journey must continue into home and family life.

Although most of what has been described so far is pertinent for use in a church context, the importance of family to a child's faith journey should not be underestimated. For full effectiveness, what is played out in church must be echoed at home. Since we are looking particularly at Holy Communion, it is interesting to note that liturgists such as Louis Weil have connected the rituals of family meals with parallels in Holy Communion rituals.[9] It is fascinating to see how families have built their own rituals around mealtimes and how these rituals, in their own way, speak into the themes we have drawn out of 'special meals', being part of God's family, showing God's love to others and 'remembering'.

Here are some practical snapshots of how families are using mealtime prayers and rituals with their young children, as told by readers of the Flame: Creative Children's Ministry blog:

9. Louis Weil, *Children and Worship* in D. Apostolos-Cappadona (Ed.), *The Sacred Play of Children*, (New York: Seabury Press, 1983), page 59.

Bonnie Thomson: We use a clapping prayer to say grace each night, to the song 'Thank you, Lord, for giving us food'. Our 1-year-old will clap along to it and says 'amen' at the end.

Kate Mitchell: During Advent we had an Advent candle which we lit each day at the dinner table and we would have 20-30 seconds of silence as we looked at the candle. The children were 1 and 3 years old. The 1-year-old wasn't always silent, but we certainly got that sense of a 'moment of wonder'. Most days we would then have a conversation about things we were grateful for or people we wanted to pray for.

Nicole Hall: What worked for us was making place mats with prayer prompts and using them at the table to help with prayers.

Judy Heron-Graham: We always have a candle on the dinner table in the liturgical colour of the day. Also place mats the colour of the liturgical season. The kids would notice the change of colour, e.g. one day white in August and they would ask why, and we could then tell the story of the transfiguration.

Lisa Marie: We pray before meals but if my 2-year-old gets seconds and it's hot, he tells us we need to pray again (while his food cools down).

Ramona Samuel: We have done a 'thankfulness' jar where each person puts in things that happen throughout the year for which they are thankful; then we read them out at the end of the year. We try to have daily devotions and the kids would read from the Bible (now we use a Bible app). We say a simple prayer at mealtimes: 'Father, thank you for the food. Amen.'

Caroline Prest: We chose six favourite tunes e. g. 'Row, row, row your boat' and made up funny 'grace' songs for each. We then labelled a small square box on each side with a different song. We would then throw it each dinner time to see which grace to sing. We still sing one now and my lot have entered their teens.

Marcus Hockley: We say grace as a family and when our 5-month-old is older we'll teach him various grace songs I learned while growing up. We also share prayer requests and then pray for each other on Saturday night. This helps us to develop confidence in praying out loud and for others.

Martha Hubbard Miller: We celebrate baptism birthdays at dinner on that day. The ritual includes lighting a candle that has the person's initials on it, letting them wear a cross necklace made of shells, and reading together about the day of the Baptism (which includes a church bulletin and the signatures of those who made promises on that day).

Rachel Shilling: We had a box of photos of family members, godparents, friends etc. that we would take one out of and pray a simple prayer for. We also used a rock, cross or the willow tree praying girl to pass around the table or floor for the next person to pray.

Food will always be an important part of our life together and there is an abundance of opportunity for helping children to make connections between the special meal we celebrate as the family of God and the meals we celebrate as a domestic family. In each case there is reverence, fellowship and celebration of God and his story.

As always, there is something important about looking to tradition as we explore rituals and celebrations within the family. Instead of inventing the wheel, how can we learn from and build on something that is already used and valued?

Here is the story of how one Christian family has drawn on the Jewish tradition of a weekly Shabbat meal and has been able to engage their young children in the rituals and symbols of this special meal with God at the centre.

Case Study:
Victoria Beech, Shabbat

We celebrate Shabbat every Friday evening by saying various blessings, prayers and simple rituals using candles, water, bread and wine.

We started 10 years ago having read about it in a book called 'How to be a Jew'. I read the chapter on Shabbat and was so moved that I wrote thousands of words about it, then three days later we did our first Shabbat. And we have done it every Friday since!

Our children are included fundamentally. This is a ritual for all of us, just as the meal is for all of us. They have always been present at the table with us, and had their first solid food as part of Shabbat. They've washed their hands when we do ours as part of a 'sorry' ritual. They sometimes break the bread and they join in with various blessings. When they were born we shortened the whole ritual from about 30 minutes to 10, and sometimes we serve food before the prayers as they need to eat! I also changed many of the Bible verses to a more child-friendly version and wrote songs for some of the Bible verses and blessings which we all sing.

It's important to our family because it's the most important part of our week, it's the place where we meet God together, thank and praise him, and acknowledge our full dependence on him for everything. We don't book anything else on that night and we celebrate it wherever we are. If we have other people with us, we invite them to join us.

Our children have demonstrated connection with God through the physical rituals since before they could explain their faith verbally to us. I remember my daughter sitting with her hands in the water having a silent moment with God for ages one time. She just paused and focused in such a way that it was clear something was happening for her.

However parents choose to create rituals in the home, the important thing is that children are encouraged to see that God does not stay behind the church door. God is with them at home and wherever they go and belonging to the family of God is as much about their identity at home as it is at church.

With that in mind, here are some practical, easy suggestions to help parents and carers explore and establish some meal time rituals:

- Create a set of graces to use before you eat. You might want to make a cube out of card and write one on each face and use it as a 'Grace cube'. Throw the cube and pray whichever grace lands face up.

- Light a candle before the meal starts and ask children to remember one person they would like God to bless and help.

- Print off and use the 'Thank you, God, for . . .' grace place mat. Ask children to choose one of the symbols and thank God for that thing before the meal starts, e.g. 'Thank you, God, for food, especially pizza'.

- Print off and use the 'Grace' play dough mat. Choose one of the graces and sing or say it before you start your meal.

- Choose a familiar song (e.g. a nursery rhyme and make up a simple grace to sing to that tune).

- Once a week, read a Bible story to the children before you eat and use the meal time to discuss it.

- Light a candle before you start your meal to remind you that Jesus, the light of the world, is with you as you eat.

- Choose some people to pray for and add a stone or shell to a special bowl for each person.

- Once a week have a 'celebration' meal where everyone wears something particularly nice, the table is set with special plates and a favourite prayer is said. Use the time to talk about all the good things that have happened that week and say thank you to God.

- Go to a 'paint a pot' shop and create a special plate or cup for each member of the family to be used in a celebration meal.

Useful books and other resources:

- **Shabbat Family Service Sheet**, available via www.godventure.co.uk
  Victoria Beech

- **Our Family Godventure**, available via www.godventure.co.uk
  Victoria Beech

- **Faithful Families: Creating Sacred Moments at Home**
  Traci Smith, (Chalice Press, 2017).

Useful websites:

- **Godventure**: www.godventure.co.uk
- **Kate Milosovic**: https://missionmummy.com
- **Faith 5**: http://www.faith5.org
- **Faith in Homes**: www.faithinhomes.co.uk
- **Practicing Families**: http://www.practicingfamilies.com
- **Traci Smith** (Faithful Families) www.traci-smith.com
- **For a collection of graces to familiar tunes**:
  http://www.guidinguk.com/graces.html

   72

Chapter 8

Downloadable resources

Download from:
https://www.kevinmayhew.com/we-all-share.html

Communion Symbols Game

Print out two copies of this sheet and glue card onto the back of each. Cut out each rectangle to make picture cards. Lay the cards face down so the pictures are hidden. Children take it in turns to turn over two cards. If they pick a matching pair they can keep them. If not, turn them over and let the next person try. The person who has the most cards at the end of the game is the winner.

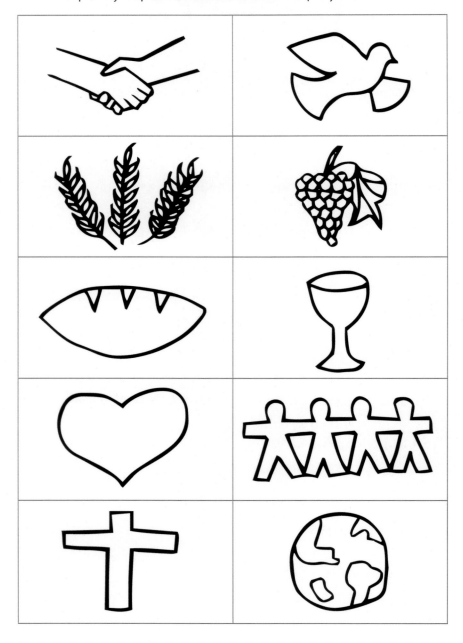

I am part of God's big family

God's big family

Use play dough to fill in the people and heart shapes

Think about who is in your family

Say thank you to God

for people you love

remember me

At a special meal,
Jesus asked his disciples
to remember him.

Use play dough to make
a cup and some bread in
these shapes.

What is your
special meal?

Use play dough
to make it on
this plate.

Thank you God

For food . . .

For drinks . . .

For people . . .

(Choose something or someone to say thank you to God for.

For the world . . .

82

Grace

For our food,
for our food,
we thank you,
we thank you.
Help us share with others. (x2)
Amen, Amen.

(Frère Jacques)

Thank you for drinks . . .
Thank you for friends . . .
Thank you for food . . . .

Amen.

Thank you, God, for food you give,
helping us to play and live.
Thank you, God, for family.
Thank you, God, for loving me.
Thank you, God, for all my friends.
Thank you, God, Amen, Amen.

(Twinkle, twinkle, little star)

Print this out,
stick it on to thin card,
then cut it out and
glue the cube together.

Roll the cube and pray
whatever lands face up.

Prayer Cube

Take Home Sheets

HOLY COMMUNION TAKE HOME 1

Memory Box

Today we have been talking about 'remembering' and why we remember Jesus during Communion. This activity can be done at home to help your child to build on this theme.

You will need:

- A plastic take away/ sandwich box
- Stickers to decorate
- Memory items to put in the box

What to do:

- Decorate the box with stickers.
- Find items that hold particular memories of p... put them into the box, e.g. photos, small toys
- Let your child share the contents of the box about why these memories are important t...

HOLY COMMUNION TAKE HOME 2

A Special Meal

Today we have been talking about Holy Communion as a special meal. Here is a recipe you can bake with your child at home and use to talk about special food your family eats or special meals you have together.

Simple Scones

Ingredients:
- 100g self-raising flour
- 30g butter
- Milk to mix
- Tablespoon sugar
- Pinch of salt
- 1 Egg

- Preheat the oven to 180° C.
- Rub the butter into the flour until it resembles breadcrumbs.
- Mix in the sugar and salt.
- Gradually add milk to the mixture until a dough is formed. Don't let it get too sticky!
- Roll out the dough until it is about 3 cm thick. Use a cutter to cut round shapes (the dough will make about 6).
- Place on a greased baking tray.
- Whisk an egg and use a pastry brush to 'wash' it over the top of each circle.
- Bake scones for 10 minutes until golden.
- Leave to cool and then eat with butter and jam!

© 2012 Kevin Mayhew Ltd. 1914736

TaKe Home Sheets

HOLY COMMUNION TAKE HOME 3

Belonging to God's Family

Today we talked about Holy Communion being a s...
family and that everyone is welcome to be part of...
dough mat to help children to explore this idea.

You will need:

- A laminated play dough mat, play dough

Follow the instructions on the play dough mat an...
what it means to be in a family and why God's f...

What is it like to be in God's family?

HOLY COMMUNION TAKE HOME 4

Sharing God's Love

Today we talked about the theme of Jesus loving us and wanting us to share that love with others. Here is a prayer activity you can do with things you will find at home.

You will need:

- Cups with about an inch of water at the bottom
- Strips of kitchen roll (about an inch wide)
- Felt tip pens (cheap and cheerful are good and definitely not permanent markers – you need the ink to run!)

Instructions:

- Draw a heart about 2 inches from the bottom of the strip and colour in with pen.
- Close to the heart (but not inside it) write the initials of someone (or draw a face of someone!) that you sometimes find it tricky to love – maybe because you don't get on very well.
- Put the end of the strip in the water and pray that God will help you to show that person that you love them and that God loves them.
- Watch as the water slowly climbs up the strip and the ink in the heart spreads out to cover and absorb the initials. This is a symbol of how you want your love and God's love to reach out to that person.

How to Sheets

HOW TO MAKE
Scented Play Dough

You will need:
- 2 cups plain flour
- 2 tablespoons vegetable oil
- 1 cup of salt
- 1.5 cups of boiling water
- 2 tablespoons cream of tartar
- 2 different types of food colouring
- 2 different baking 'essences' e.g. peppermint, lemon, almond

Instructions:
- Mix the flour, oil, salt and cream of tartar.
- Gradually add the boiling water until the mixture starts to hang together as a dough.
- Leave in the bowl to cool.
- Take the dough out of the mixing bowl and knead it for a few minutes. Add more flour if it is too sticky.
- Split the dough into two pieces.
- Put a few drops of your first food colouring onto o... then add a few drops of your first essence.
- Knead the colour and essence into the dough u...
- Repeat with your second piece of play dough, adding a different colour and a different essen...

You will now have two different scented doughs!

Alternatively, make one scented dough by addin... when you add the boiling water.

HOW TO MAKE
Body of Christ Crayons

You will need:
- Silicone moulds for making ice cubes or chocolates
  (If you use ice cube moulds check that they will withstand the temperature of the oven.) I used a mould that made mini-people shapes but you could use any shape you want.
- 2 packs of wax crayons
- An oven

Instructions:
- Preheat your oven to 200°C.
- Remove the paper from around the crayons and break them up into small pieces.
- Get the children to fill the moulds with a mixture of different coloured pieces of crayon. Don't fill the moulds right to the top or you may have spillage!
- Put the mould into the oven and bake for between 5 and 8 minutes.
- Keep an eye on the melting crayons and when it looks like they have all melted and there are no more lumps, take the mould out of the oven.
- Let the shapes cool and then take them out of the mould.

You will have a shape made up of lots of different pieces!